POEMS FOR THE CHURCH'S YEAR

Copyright © 2013 by Richard France
All rights reserved

ISBN-13: 978-1480269217

ISBN-10: 1480269212

LCCN 2012923784

CreateSpace Independent Publishing Platform

North Charleston, SC

CONTENTS

Advent	7
Advent – Carols	8
Christmas – The Shepherds	9
Christmas – The Shepherds' Farewell	10
Christmastide	11
The Epiphany – Mary	12
The Epiphany – The Wise Men	14
The Baptism of the Lord	16
The Presentation – Nunc Dimittis	18
The Annunciation – Magnificat	19
The Visitation – Benedictus	21
Ash Wednesday	22
Holy Thursday – The Last Supper	23
Holy Thursday – Gethsemane	24
Good Friday – When Jesus Died	25
Good Friday – Why Did Jesus Die?	26
Good Friday – The Good Thief	28
Good Friday – The Way of the Cross	29
Holy Saturday – The Mourners	33
The Easter Vigil	34
The Dawning of Easter	36
Easter Morning – Sorrow turned to Joy	38
Easter Morning – The Empty Tomb	40
Low Sunday	43
The Ascension – An Angel's-eye-view	46
The Journey to Pentecost	47

Pentecost – The Upper Room	49
The Sacred Heart	53
The Transfiguration	54
The Assumption	56
All Saints – Sharing The Victory	57
Christ the King	58

PREFACE

The aim of these poems is to show how much life is represented by the Church's Year. References such as 'Cycle C' in a church newsletter might, at first, sound like technical terms; perhaps, though, 'Cycles' can be seen as different sources of light being shone on a subject – the subject in this case being the lives of God's people.

Some of the poems are partly conjecture, but usually conjecture which is based on the facts recorded in the gospels. For instance, no-one may know how Mary Magdalen – one of the most intriguing characters in the New Testament – reacted when she met Jesus after the Resurrection. Nevertheless, her presence at the Crucifixion is described, and gives an indication of the contrast between what probably were her emotions then – utter devastation – and her joy later on, when she met the risen Christ. As a result, what she, and other people, said and did can be guessed fairly accurately.

So these poems are only depictions of the *way* things might have happened. However, many incredible things *did* happen. Events such as the Birth, Passion, Death, Resurrection, and Ascension of Christ are all beyond question; they – together with the Love of Christ – make up the truth we believe in. Some may, from time to time, find this truth too good to believe. But then, as they say, truth is stranger than fiction.

R.F.

ADVENT

For five and twenty days – or thereabouts -
We can prepare our hearts, repent, and wait.
We can rejoice as well – Christ will be born
In us, on that day we anticipate.

And surely this is what we all wait for,
The reason why we have prepared the way –
So Christ can come once more into our hearts,
His love transforming our night into day.

A few weeks only, that is all there is,
A time to cultivate the heart and mind,
To make a place for Jesus Christ to come
And enter in, a dwelling-place to find.

A brief time for us to accomplish all
The things we have to do – but then we know
How long we have, the date by which we will
Have finished running round, and to and fro.

A longer wait we have until the time,
When He will come again – and come He will,
In glory and in power – but will we
Be ready, praying, trusting, loving, still?

ADVENT – Carols

Sounds of joy that bring to mind
That wondrous night, long, long ago,
When Jesus came to humankind,
When heaven looked on earth below,

When angels glorified their king,
Our Saviour, in a stable laid,
Sang melodies that we might sing,
To imitate the song they made.

Carried on the cold night air,
Sung by the fireside at home,
Or else inside a church somewhere,
Perhaps beneath a splendid dome,

Such simple and yet special notes,
Make up the carol's joyful sound
Which, like the lightest feather floats
Upon the air, and echoes round.

Played on a tape, or by a band,
In theatres, or in concert-halls;
And everywhere, throughout the land,
The Christmas carol ever calls

The world to stop, and pause, and rest –
To think "Who gave us Christmas cheer?"
So every Christmas-time is blessed
With carols, sung anew, each year.

CHRISTMAS – The Shepherds

The shepherds at the manger stood
In wonder and in awe,
And looked upon the child,
As He lay there, on the straw.

And though they could have stayed, adored
The One they saw asleep,
Yet they in time had to return
To guard and tend their sheep.

Now they are dead, they who adored,
Who at the crib did pray;
Although the child, Christ, lives on
Here, in the Mass each day.

Gold, frankincense, and myrrh have gone,
And they have been replaced;
With bread and wine and water now,
New cribs have all been graced.

Though that first Christmas is long gone,
Those shepherds have all died,
Yet now new shepherds take their place,
With new sheep by their side.

Not round the manger do they stand,
But round the altar, where
Christ is still brought to us anew,
Adored, and worshipped there.

CHRISTMAS – The Shepherds' Farewell

The shepherds gazed into skies above,
And marvelled at the light the heavens gave –
The stars, created by the Lord of love,
Born on that night, the Christ who came to save.

No shelter but a cave served as a place
Where the exhausted mother could give birth,
A cave – it was not much, but was a space,
One where the Son of God could come on earth.

They looked down from the hillside far below:
Beside a crib, two figures knelt in prayer;
Their cave, lit by the light of Christ, a glow,
A distant glow – but they had all been there,

And had at last returned to tend their sheep,
Still looking back, while waiting for the dawn;
It was a memory that they would keep,
A blessed night – that night when Christ was born.

CHRISTMASTIDE

It is a sacred, precious time of year:
Though all seems finished, over put away,
The holy tide of Christmas is still here,
For Christmastide begins on Christmas Day!

And Christmas does not simply just consist
Of Advent's end, and after that, no more –
For Christ is born anew within our hearts,
Calls to us now, to life for evermore.

And so there is the time of Christmastide,
To celebrate the news that Christmas brings;
We have these grace-filled, and God-given days,
To ponder on such great and mighty things.

Reflecting, just as Mary did, upon
The time that she herself had known before:
Days when, they said, there was no after-life,
Days without hope – these were now no more.

For Christ was born, and with Him He would bring
New hope, and share their suffering and strife,
Tell of God's mercy, and then show the way
To God, to heaven, and eternal life.

THE EPIPHANY – Mary

She watched, as from their camels they now all
Alighted. Mary gazed then at each one:
Saw each one pause, look at the manger, fall
Upon his knees, to worship Christ, her Son.

They came with gifts – why gifts? – yet these they brought,
Sweet frankincense, and myrrh, and gifts of gold,
As if it were a king whom they had sought.
But had they carried these throughout the cold,

Dark desert nights? Across the windswept plain?
While resting only in the noonday heat?
At least, their journey had not been in vain.
Who were they? And then how should she now greet

These men who came here – and how had they found
This place? Had they looked everywhere on earth?
Why did they all bow low, down to the ground,
Almost as though they knew of Jesus' birth?

But more than this, as they stayed deep in prayer,
She wondered at the silence and the peace;
The joy they showed to see the infant there,
A joy she shared, and wished would never cease.

Though what had moved them so, to travel here?
What certainty had made them all decide
To leave their homes? And why did they appear
So glad, content and joyful? Mary tried

To think why Jesus touched their hearts this way,
What was it prompted them to lay before
Him all their gifts? Why was it? Could she say?
Yet they would be remembered evermore.

THE EPIPHANY – The Wise Men

The wise men rode to Bethlehem,
Each bringing gifts that day,
And offered them to Christ the Lord,
Where He slept in the hay.

The first wise man now brought with him
A sacred offering,
To Him whom they had longed to see,
To Jesus, Christ the King.

A gift he offered so that all
Christ's kingship might behold,
The treasure that he brought that night –
A gift made all of gold.

The second man had brought a gift,
Which was in turn unsealed;
A gift which, offered to the Christ,
His Godhead now revealed.

The man brought with him frankincense –
The gift could not be priced –
And as it burned, its fragrance filled
The birthplace of the Christ.

But then the third man offered up
The gift that he had brought:
No frankincense, no gift of gold,
For Him who he had sought –

The bitter perfume of the myrrh,
As if to prophesy
The passion Christ would undergo,
The death that He would die.

But then those wise men went away –
Wise, for their deeds did show
That they had offered all to God –
And homeward now did go.

THE BAPTISM OF THE LORD

He had a mission, which was to prepare
The way, for One who would come from on high;
There was a message which he had to bear
And, in the wilderness, was heard his cry:

"Convert your lives and change your hearts! Repent!
The time you have been waiting for draws near!"
And those who heard him hurried, all intent
On learning of the One who would appear.

They gathered by the Jordan everyday,
To be baptised by John, who called them there,
To change their lives, and follow in the way
He showed them. So they all went down to where

John stood. And then into the river each
Would go, and wait there, while the waters swirled
Around them, while John they would beseech
"Who is this, who will come to save the world?"

And as he taught them, as the Baptist poured
Clean water over each and every one,
Fresh hope was born in them, their spirits soared
Because, for them, a new life had begun.

But then John saw One who towards him came
Along the desert path, that he first trod,
Whose presence he could now to all proclaim:
John's voice rang out, "Here comes the Lamb of God!"

THE PRESENTATION – Nunc Dimittis

The old priest watched the couple who drew near,
Two turtle-doves they brought – so they were poor,
But still, a spotless lamb would cost them dear…
He smiled. It was in keeping with the Law!

He looked again, his old eyes weary now,
And in the woman's arms he saw the child –
A child that he recognised somehow,
What made the child special? Once more he smiled,

And then his age-worn eyes were filled with tears
Of joy, and pleasure, of that special kind,
That only comes with waiting many years,
Joy, which for him would now be unconfined.

For there, held in the mother's arms he saw
The one he had for so long, now, expected.
He knew though, that it was not long before
He, who would save the world, would be rejected.

Until he saw the Christ, he had been told –
For God had made it known – he would not die.
He had been praying, until he grew old,
But now at last could go, to God on high.

THE ANNUNCIATION – Magnificat

What was the light she saw? Whose face was there?
She gazed. Who was that, dressed in shining white?
A silver belt around the waist, the hair
Of burning gold, the eyes so clear and bright?

Was this…an angel, with a flowing cloak?
She felt the presence, next looked at the face,
And waited, while the one she saw now spoke.
She trembled at the greeting: 'Hail, full of grace!'

What did it mean? Who could be full of grace?
Grace was a gift that only God could give!
So who was this? And was God in this place ?
Had He come down here from on high, to live?

The hopes that God would, one day, come to earth
She shared – God's Word she knew, and did believe –
But had she thought who would bring Him to birth?
Or of the prophecy? 'A virgin will conceive…'

It was too much, and yet the words were clear –
And spoken to her, '…you shall bear a Son,'
It was God's will, there was no room for fear,
Salvation, and new life, had now begun.

A joy so great she simply had to share,
But how? What could she say? Who could she tell?
That she – unmarried – would a child bear,
That through her, God would come down here to dwell?

The angel's voice now calmed her troubled mind,
"Elizabeth, your cousin, is with child,
Go to her and you will a welcome find,"
And Mary listened, pondered, and then smiled.

She set out, for the journey would be long,
And strewn with rocks and boulders on the way,
And so much, so it seemed, that could go wrong -
But still, why did the joy within her stay?

A joy so glorious and so sublime –
Was God's great plan achieved through her somehow?
Had all the prophets spoken of this time?
Was this the day, was this the moment, now?

As soon as she arrived, her cousin knew:
At once called her 'the mother of my Lord.'
So... all the angel said was really true!
And Mary's joy now overflowed, and poured

Out from her heart, now with God's love aflame,
Into a song of blessing, thanks, and praise,
Which grew, so that it magnified God's name,
Rejoicing in the wonder of His ways.

THE VISITATION – Benedictus

He sat there, heard them ask "What name shall he
Be called?" He looked on, powerless. They turned
Towards him – all still unaware how he
Must feel, as his heart within him burned.

His child's name had to be chosen now,
The mother and her friends all gathered round;
They should consult the father – but then how?
A slate for him to write on must be found.

Since that dread day the angel struck him dumb,
Strange mixed emotions had torn him apart;
First fear, humiliation, and then hope,
Joy, understanding, flowed into his heart.

An understanding of God's mighty plan,
From endless ages to this very day,
How his own son would later be the man
Who, for the Most High, would prepare the way.

And who besides him knew this? Who indeed?
News of redemption, that he longed to share,
To tell his family – and he would need
To give his son the message he must bear.

This was his chance. The boy would be called John,
Just as the angel said. He wrote the name.
Then speech returned – all he had dwelt upon
Poured out – and from deep in his heart it came.

ASH WEDNESDAY

We often stray – and there's a cost,
We on the storms of life are tossed,
Where are we now? For we are lost!
"Have mercy on us, Lord, for we have sinned."

Upon life's journey we depart,
And on our way we may lose heart,
Oh bring us back, Lord, to the start,
"Have mercy on us Lord, for we have sinned."

And our mistakes will often mar
The plans we make, which would go far –
Remind us, Lord, just who we are,
"Have mercy on us, Lord, for we have sinned."

We hold you in our hearts each day,
We try to do our best to pray,
Oh, tell us what we need to say,
"Have mercy on us, Lord, for we have sinned."

We seek the things which should be sought,
We try to do the things we ought,
Yet when our efforts come to nought,
"Have mercy on us, Lord, for we have sinned."

HOLY THURSDAY – The Last Supper

"I will be with you always," said the Lord,
"Though I shall go, and leave all of you here;
So with this Eucharist you will give thanks,
And when you do, you need have no more fear,

For, in those moments, I will come to live
Within the bread, which shall become for you
The bread of life, my life, which you will share,
And so what I have done, you too must do.

And just as I walked with you in the streets,
Among the hills, beneath the open sky,
Or through the desert with its dust and stones,
Or in Jerusalem – fear not, for I

Shall be with you, and others down the years,
And with the life I give, you shall be fed;
So call to me, and I will come to you,
When you, with me, and others, share this bread."

HOLY THURSDAY – Gethsemane

He felt the weight of sin upon him now,
That sin of Adam, who had spurned God's love,
Though given all the gifts God could bestow,
And all that God could shower from above;

Had known the joy that always could be found,
When he obeyed God's will, and not his own –
Before the Fall, there was no sin around –
And Adam walked with God, and Him alone.

And yet, despite this, he was not content –
Rejected God, when given his free will;
But Christ, on saving him was still intent
And, praying in the garden, loved him still.

The more He loved, the more He suffered, though,
With such great love, He suffered all the more;
While Sin now fell on Jesus like a blow,
And added to the burden which He bore.

And often Adam's children down the years
Had turned their backs on God, and they had strayed
Far from the path of life – and so brought tears
To Jesus, in the garden, where he prayed.

Deserted by His friends and left alone,
The cup of suffering he now accepted.
And for the sins of all He would atone.
So finally, God's Son had been rejected.

GOOD FRIDAY – When Jesus Died

God loved the world that He had made
And we, who lived in it, were free.
God rescued us when we had strayed,
So Jesus died, for you and me.

He taught us how to live, to love,
Not thinking of ourselves – to be
Prepared to follow him above –
And so He died, for you and me.

He was God, but to those in power,
A threat to their authority,
He had to die – this was His hour –
When Jesus died, for you and me.

He made no noise – there was no need –
But patiently hung there, so He
Could die for us, and then could lead
The way to life, for you and me.

So He, our Lord, was left to die,
Was crucified upon that tree,
But rose to life, ascended high,
And now He lives, for you and me.

GOOD FRIDAY – Why Did Jesus Die?

Why did He die? So all of us who die,
Who've followed Him, will never die in vain;
We will be dying just as Jesus died,
And, just like Jesus, we will rise again.

Why did He die? Because that was the price,
That Jesus had to pay, upon the tree;
So Jesus had to sacrifice Himself,
To suffer, and to die, for you and me.

Why did He die? That was the reason why
He came down from His home in heaven above;
He loved us all, but then there was a cost –
So Jesus had to pay the price of love.

Why did He die? He died to conquer sin,
To save us all from Satan, and from hell;
As we died, in the world that we were in,
To be like us, He had to die as well.

Why did He die? To open up the way,
The way to heaven. His death was the price.
But others tried to stop Him, so He had
To make for us the eternal sacrifice.

His mother, John, and Mary Magdalen,
For three hours or more of silence stood nearby;
Just seven times they all three heard Him speak,
And at the end, they heard Him give a cry:

'Forgive them,' 'Today you shall be with me,'
'O God, my God,' and then 'This is your son.'
'I thirst,' 'It is accomplished,' finally,
'Into your hands,' so victory He won.

GOOD FRIDAY – The Good Thief

"They caught me, hung me on a cross,
Yet how can I complain?
Since I am paying for my crime,
And I must bear the pain.

But Jesus, You are here as well,
Why are You crucified?
Why do You suffer like me, Lord?
Yet You are by my side.

And though You had brought joy to lives,
And hope, where all else failed,
Yet You were made to bear a cross,
And to it You were nailed.

And You, so I can be redeemed,
Remain upon the cross;
You have restored to me once more
All I had counted loss.

You show the way to paradise,
Reversing my despair,
Speak to me of a life to come,
While You are hanging there.

Now all I have to do is stay
Upon the cross, with You;
Then dwell with You, in paradise,
And always be with You."

GOOD FRIDAY – The Way Of The Cross

The soldiers brought the man held bound
Before the governor's chair;
He made no sound as He looked around
At His accusers there.

The governor said He should not die,
But the crowd around him surged,
Then he heard the cry of "Crucify!"
And he said He must be scourged.

They tore His clothes, so His back lay bare,
To a pillar His hands they tied,
They whipped Him there, yet unaware
That justice had been denied.

A king, the Man had claimed to be,
That much the governor knew;
He thought that he should set Him free -
But what was he to do?

"No king of ours!" at once they said,
But with thorns they made a crown,
And Jesus bled, as on His head
They fiercely thrust it down.

None knew the truth, but for a jest
A purple robe they found;
In it they dressed the One so blessed,
That King, so cruelly crowned.

And next they placed into His hand
Instead of a sceptre, a reed;
They mocked the Man, and made Him stand,
They struck Him, and watched Him bleed.

The soldiers then upon Him laid
A cross that bowed Him down,
And though it weighed so much, they made
Him carry it through the town.

He met His mother, who gave one
Deep and heart-rending sigh –
Saw what they'd done to her dear son,
Now on His way to die.

Afraid that too soon He might die,
Beneath that cross so great,
The soldiers spied a man close by,
And made him share the weight.

One who looked on, now left her place
She came – no sound was heard –
With quiet grace, wiped Jesus' face
Then left, without a word.

Pierced by those thorns He freely bled,
Yet did not weaken till
He looked ahead, with fear and dread,
As He approached the hill.

Twice He stumbled, on the way,
He could not see so well,
Those thorns now tore into Him more –
And then once more He fell.

The women who beheld His plight
Saw all the hopes they'd kept,
Now put to flight – it seemed a light
Had gone out – and they wept.

He said "though you all weep for me,
For Jerusalem I mourn,
So it must be – meanwhile I see
Your hearts with sorrow torn."

So He continued on His way,
And now began the climb,
But on the way, once more that day
He fell – a final time.

And at the summit, they now ripped
Away the clothes He wore;
He had been whipped, so when they stripped
Him, Jesus' back was raw.

Then down upon the Cross they made
Him lie, and nailed Him there,
And there He stayed, beyond all aid,
His only refuge – prayer.

The sun now faded, it grew dark
Across the barren sky,
While those who loved Him, and stood near,
Saw Jesus, raised on high,
They heard His tears, they heard His prayers,
They wept, and watched Him die.

A soldier's lance then pierced His side,
And Blood and Water came;
From Him who died, the Crucified,
Flowed life in Jesus' name.

His friends now climbed the Cross to bear
His body to the ground,
Then lowered Him there, with utmost care
And all without a sound.

They carried Him to a place nearby,
Laid Jesus in the grave;
One from on high, who came to die,
That sinners He might save.

HOLY SATURDAY – The Mourners

They grieved in silence for their loss;
Their hope, their longed-for Christ,
Had died in pain upon a cross –
Betrayed, and sacrificed.

Where hope had grown, despair now grew –
They could not bear this blow;
What would they do, what could they do,
Wherever could they go?

Crushed, broken, overwhelmed, bereft,
Confused and terrified;
With anxious hearts they now were left,
Ignored, and swept aside.

The new life that they thought they'd gained,
Had died with Christ that day;
His body was all that remained,
And in a tomb it lay.

They would anoint the body, though,
And do it all with love –
Though even the tomb was guarded now,
With orders from above.

THE EASTER VIGIL

No sound is heard, and all has stopped within
The silent church, for in there it is night.
As if surrounded by the dark of sin,
The people stand, all waiting for the light.

And now it comes – still no more than a glow –
Enough to light up all those standing near;
The Easter fire slowly starts to grow,
And soon all see a tiny flame appear.

And, still in silence, from this holy flame
Is lit the Easter candle, which will burn,
To be a sign of life in Jesus' Name.
Then from this candle other ones in turn

Are lit, as if all can new life expect;
So faces now begin to glow as they,
From candles now aflame, that life reflect –
And dark to light, and sin to grace, gives way.

But then the light of Christ is borne on high,
And carried through the church, that all may draw
New hope, from that light which will never die,
The light that will be with us evermore.

And always this tradition will go on,
Though sin and darkness try to have their way;
The conquering light is still the same that shone
When Christ arose on that first Easter Day.

THE DAWNING OF EASTER

She walked to the tomb with others that day,
To anoint the One who died,
But she said "Will the soldiers bar our way,
Or move the stone aside?"

Could she have seen what the soldiers saw,
As she drew near the tomb?
They had stood by the stone that sealed the door,
And guarded it in the gloom.

Could she have heard what the soldiers heard,
The grinding, rumbling sound?
But all was silent, and nothing stirred –
There was darkness all around.

Could she have known what the soldiers knew
The cold and trembling fear?
Looked on, as angels moved the stone,
Then seen the Christ appear?

Had she seen, shining from the tomb,
That first small ray of light?
Watched, as the stone was rolled away,
Witnessed the glorious sight?

No, she only saw two angels where
Two guards had stood that morning.
And then – Who else could she see there?
It was dark…but the day was dawning.

EASTER MORNING – Mary

Sorrow turned to joy

She remembered how she'd watched and waited, and how she had cried,
Two days ago she'd stood there, and into her arms received
The body of her child, her son, who on a cross had died…
She was exhausted from her tears, but in her heart believed

All would be well. Yet she had stayed with Him, her son so dear,
Then later she had held His lifeless body, and He lay
There in her arms – her son, God's Son, whose words still echoed clear,
"Behold your son." Who had he meant? What had He tried to say?

Those words "Behold your son", she wondered, what did He intend?
Why, Jesus was her son, and so – could he give her another?
She gazed across at John, who stood there, faithful to the end –
Saw Jesus look at John and say to him: "Behold your mother."

For God there was no gift it was impossible
to give,
She saw it now, so this son, John, would
calm her hopes and fears –
Fears for the children yet unborn, her hopes
that they might live
And, just like John beneath the cross, stay
faithful down the years.

For those children, she now saw, God had
entrusted to her care,
His life would be in them, her children, each
and every one;
So she, their mother, she would love those
children, everywhere,
And lead them all to Jesus. As Mary walked
there in the sun

She sighed, and she remembered how the
Word grew in her heart:
How God chose her, to let the Word take
flesh, and let Him grow,
And live at Nazareth with her, and Joseph, start
To gather followers, and live, and die – two
days ago.

She sighed – then all at once rejoiced, for she
saw far away,
God's plan unfolding, people running, their
voices loud and strong;
Mary guessed their news: "the tomb is empty,"
they would say,
Then " Jesus Christ is risen!" – and yes – joy
 was all their song.

EASTER MORNING – The Empty Tomb

I found the tomb empty, though I had come there
To anoint the Lord's body – then saw it was gone;
So I, Mary Magdalen, in my despair,
Had turned to the gardener, then I went on:

"Tell me, O gardener, tell me, I pray,
What was it you saw when you came to the tomb?
You are here before dawn at your work every day,
So what did you see in the dark and the gloom?

Long before sunrise you must have been here,
For you come at the earliest time of the day,
O tell me, who else was it came to the garden –
O, who stole my Lord, and then took Him away?

His body is sacred to those whom He loved,
And if we can find it, then we shall all weep
Loving tears, for then we can anoint our dear Lord –
But until we have done so, then we shall not sleep!

So tell me please, who was it came here by night,
Placed Him somewhere they thought He would never be found?
And tell me, too, who was it struck both the guards,
Who are motionless lying down there on the ground?

Tell me, O gardener, if you were here,
Before I discovered you standing alone,
Did you see who it was, who came into the garden –
And if you did, tell me then, who moved the stone?"

But all I could hear was the sound of my voice
– And the silence. The gardener said not a word,
Except "Mary." But why did my heart then rejoice?
Because…who had spoken? And who had I heard?

I looked up – a dawning awareness now grew;
…No, He couldn't be here! – I was there when He died…
…But He'd said… "I will rise again," and so…it was true…
In joy and elation "Rabboni!" I cried,

And I fell at His feet, overcome with relief,
For I felt in that instant new hope and new love,
Which I never had known in my sorrow and grief,
And I felt a new faith – it had come from above.

I would go and find Peter to tell him the news,
That the One we had lost, and thought buried and gone,
And all we believed, and we thought was no more –
Had come back! And all Jesus began would go on!

The Lord's promises made to us were not in vain;
So I'd run to tell Peter – and others I'd tell –
"All we thought we had lost will be ours, once again,
Christ is risen! And with us! Yes, all will be well!"

LOW SUNDAY

When Thomas saw the suffering, the evil all around,
In order to believe, he had to know the reason why –
When would the kingdom be restored? Would Jesus then be crowned?
What had He meant by saying He 'must suffer and then die?'

But Thomas heard that He had suffered, heard that Christ had died,
Whatever he had once believed, he had believed in vain;
The One who once worked miracles had since been crucified,
So evil had now triumphed, and so evil would remain.

And what could he believe in now? For what hope was there left?
He could not face the evil, and yet where was there to go?
He who had said "I am the Way" was no more, He was dead.
Now what was there that he could do? He simply did not know.

Then being told Christ was alive, doubt only he displayed.
Had Christ then risen from the dead as He had prophesied?
Still, first he had to see the wounds, the marks the nails made,
And only then would he believe that death itself had died.

But no-one could rise from the dead. So Thomas gave a sigh –
Yes, Jesus had raised Lazarus, that much of course was true –
But... Jesus had been nailed to a cross, and left to die.
So, Thomas thought, that was the end – but now what should he do?

He walked towards the Upper Room, and as he climbed the stair,
Joy, unbelief, and fear all fought together in his mind;
He waited in that room, and wondered: who would join them there?
Who had his friends all seen, and who could he expect to find?

Next 'Peace be with you,' came the voice – that voice he knew so well,
And Thomas then saw Jesus, looking straight into his eyes,
At once his fears all fled away, moreover he could tell
That evil had been conquered, and his fears he could despise.

So his fear had fled away but…what was it that still stayed?
He looked once more at Jesus, and he saw those hands and feet,
Where men had crucified Him, all the marks the nails made –
Heard once more 'Peace be with you,' – so his joy was now complete.

THE ASCENSION

An Angel's-eye View

"Why are you looking upward,
O men of Galilee?
For Jesus has ascended as you saw.
In heaven now He dwells,
With the Spirit and the Father,
And He will reign with them for evermore.

Why are you looking upward,
O men of Galilee?
Because if you seek Jesus,
To heaven He is gone.
But what you seek, your faith will find,
There, in His word and sacrament,
And in the Eucharist He left behind.

Why are you looking upward, O men of
Galilee?
For though He may be hidden,
And concealed by the clouds,
You can be very sure He is there.

For He, whom you no longer see,
Shall yet return, that you should know;
Will come to take you back with Him –
To heaven, to your home –
Will come again, just as you saw Him go."

THE JOURNEY TO PENTECOST

Merchants came from far-off western lands,
In ships of different sizes they now sailed
Across the Great Sea, to Jerusalem,
Through storms, and mists, and heat waves, they prevailed.

And others, by the ancient Incense Route,
From India, and Arabia as well;
All these brought spices, gold, and precious stones,
Which in Jerusalem they hoped to sell.

Traders from Persian lands – these travelled, too,
With silks and sandalwood come from the east,
And to Jerusalem they journeyed now –
Some said it would be busy, with the Feast.

Once there, with precious cargoes, cloth, tin, wine,
They met together in the marketplace,
Exchanging news and stories, money, goods,
Religions too, or customs of their race.

Then, just when they had come together there,
They stopped, for all of them had heard a sound,
But not a sound that they had heard before –
They stood there, speechless, rooted to the ground.

And each looked at the other, wondering,
Then heard a strong wind blowing through the air –
Yet did not feel it – and all was still,
As silently they watched, and waited there.

Then next they heard the great apostle's voice,
The voice of Peter, reaching to them all,
And coming from the high part of the town,
So loud and clear, each one could hear him call:

"…The promise is to all those who are here,
And those who are far off, in distant lands.
So take this good news, speak to all you find,
And let them win salvation from your hands."

Then other voices they began to hear,
And their amazement could not be disguised.
"How is it," they said "we know every word?"
For each of them, his language recognised.

"We come from different places, far away –
Yet these men speak to each and every one,
A promise, from a man called Jesus Christ,
News of the victory that He has won."

In time they all returned, left for their ships,
To spread this good news over all the earth –
They would tell everyone what they had heard,
And witness how a Church was brought to birth.

PENTECOST – The Upper Room

The group of apostles were gathered in prayer,
Bartholomew, James and Matthias were there,
With Andrew, the one who saw Jesus appear
And then told the rest 'The Messiah is here!'

Simon and Jude, and then Philip were in
The same room with Matthew and Thomas the Twin.
Zebedee's sons were there too, James and John,
And Peter, the one they depended upon;

Mary, the Mother of Jesus, and some
Other women, all praying the Spirit would come.
"I can pray no longer," said Thomas at last
Nine days have now gone and my patience is past."

"Have courage said Peter, "Forget all your fear,
Remember what Jesus said, when He was here:
'Stay in Jerusalem, wait here and I
Will send you the power, that comes from on high'".

Philip then turned to him smiled and sighed
"You talk just as I did when Jesus had died."
"I understand well that you feel afraid,
Though the reason," said James, "is that you have not prayed."

Thomas stood downcast, and silent, and glum,
Take heart," whispered Mary, "the Spirit will come!"

Soon a new sense of harmony started to bind
Them all closer together, in one heart and mind;
A wonderful stillness now hung in the air –
The apostles all felt it, and soon were aware

Of a small, distant noise, far from where they all were,
Yet beckoning, and their souls started to stir.
They listened, an image began to appear –
Of a light – and the noise seemed to grow – they could hear…

Yes…a beating of wings way above, up on high,
Growing nearer, descending, down, down through the sky,
The noise became louder, the closer it came,
And it fired their hearts, and it kindled a flame,

And they all were now staring, and standing around
When – "Listen!" said Andrew, "for what is that sound?"
A rushing of wind, he at once recognised,
"It's the sound that I heard when the Lord was baptised!"

And the Spirit came down in a torrent of love,
Appearing to all as a pure white dove.
And so God's Holy Dove now passed over each one,
Completing the work that the Lord had begun;

And as it flew over each one, there it stayed
Fulfilling the promises Jesus had made,
Bestowing on each all the gifts that God gave,
Miracles, prophecy, power to save,

Healing, faith, knowledge, and wisdom to all,
The Spirit now opened their hearts to God's call,
Their tongues seemed to burn, a new power of speech,
A desire, for spreading God's Word, came to each,

Bringing to mind all that Jesus had said,
The deeds He had done, and the life He had led,
The dove brought them confidence, filled them anew
With the strength that they needed, wherever it flew.

It returned to the centre and there it remained,
Confirming them all in the gifts they had gained,
Pouring out graces of goodness and joy,
Gentleness, patience no man could destroy,

Trustfulness, self-control, love, and then peace,
Assuring them God's kingdom would never cease.
And so the apostles went forth, on their way,
Each praising the Lord for His deeds on that day.

THE SACRED HEART

Filled with compassion for His scattered sheep,
Christ calls us to Him, waiting to impart
To all who come, the stream of grace and mercy
Pouring for us, from His Sacred Heart.

The fount of living water, which we seek
Will be poured out upon us, from above,
If we will only put our trust in Him,
His Sacred Heart will hold us in His love.

Looking down upon our stricken world,
As we all come before Him with our prayer,
Christ calls to us to lose our hearts in His,
Receive from Him the love we find in there.

Let us make Christ the object of our love,
And let the love from His Heart overflow
Into our own; make Christ our hearts' desire,
Desire for such love as none can know.

THE TRANSFIGURATION

Peter, James, and John now reached the place
Where they would learn that Jesus had to die;
But, before then, would look on God's own face,
And hear His voice, as He spoke from on high.

So they had climbed up to the mountain height,
Not knowing why their Master led them there,
Quite unprepared though, for the sudden light,
And then the voice, like thunder in the air.

The voice, resounding, came down from a cloud;
A terror, and a sudden trembling seized
Them, as they heard the words, so clear and loud:
'This is My Son, in Whom I am well pleased.'

Two figures, beside Jesus, they then saw,
Then heard them – Moses and Elijah – speak
To Jesus of the trials He would bear,
His 'passing.' What was that? It sounded bleak.

But Jesus' clothes were shining, white as light,
Light such as they had never seen before!
They'd build three tabernacles on this site…
But no! What were those nail-marks that they saw?

Since He had come to them down from on high,
Not crucified, but crowned, their Lord must be!
It was too much! No, Jesus could not die!
And yet there was no doubt what they could see!

It could not be! To them it seemed that God
Had just confirmed their fears, declared that He
Was pleased now with the path that Jesus trod –
The path of suffering – no, it could not be!

Exhausted, they fell face down on the ground,
Confused and dazed by those words from on high,
They lay; then, when at last they looked around,
Saw only Jesus standing there, close by.

THE ASSUMPTION

She knew no sin, to sin was to offend
The God she loved, who chose her as the one
To bring to birth His Word, whom He would send –
Could such a mother, then, offend her Son?

Offend her Lord? So Mary had been made
Immaculate by God, and with Him one
In heart and mind. Always to God she prayed,
With Jesus by her side – prayed with her son.

For she taught Jesus how to pray, would guide
Him, stand by Him, the child of her womb.
Then He returned to heaven; she too died,
But then God could not leave her in the tomb;

Death could not keep her, whom no sin did cloy,
Who had on earth known suffering and strife,
Whose soul and body to eternal joy
Were taken up – to everlasting life.

ALL SAINTS – Sharing the Victory

The saints have run the race we run,
And overcome their cares and strife,
And fought the fight, and led the way,
Shown how to gain eternal life.

And often we can read about
The saints – and some have left us all
The written record of their lives,
The works of God that they recall.

Then they will let us share their faith,
Their fortitude, their strength of will,
Success in overcoming sin –
The prayers they made are with us still.

They faced the struggles we all face,
Knew sorrow, hardship, and despair,
And when we find we need support,
The saints of God are always there.

CHRIST THE KING

The babe who once slept in the hay,
Now sits at God's right hand today,
And He looks down upon us in
A world of sadness, and of sin:

Our ancestors from long ago
Rejected God, chose darkness, so
Their world was then ruled by the prince
Of darkness, and has been, long since.

But all are waiting for the light
Of Christ to shine into the night;
And there are many here on earth,
Who love the Lord who came to birth,

Born in a humble family,
That one day we might all be free –
Free, from that prince of darkness, for
Christ gives us hope that there is more,

A better life with Him on high,
Where we will live, and never die;
And all of those who choose the light
Of Christ, will then see no more night;

He is the Saviour of us all
Who reach out to Him, hear His call,
He is the Lord of everything,
And reigns in splendour, Christ the King!

Made in the USA
Charleston, SC
25 March 2013